# COLORADO
## *Favorite Places*
### Photographs by **STEVE TOHARI**

*Dedicated to the memory of my beloved Shetland Sheepdog WEBSTER*

Mountain Goat on Mt. Evans

 SHETLAND PRESS • Breckenridge, Colorado

Design by Steve Tohari

Text by Steve Tohari

Typesetting by Debbie Black

Photo Editing by Steve Tohari


SHETLAND PRESS

P.O. Box 5347

Breckenridge, Colorado  80424


Printed in HONG KONG


ISBN# 0-9657504-9-3 (hard cover)

ISBN# 0-9657504-8-5 (soft cover)

# PREFACE

I have roamed all over the great state of Colorado for almost 20 years - on foot, on alpine skis, and in a four-wheel drive vehicle.

There are some places that I keep going back to - those are my *Favorite Places*. Every time I go back, I see something I didn't see before, and take new pictures.

The color photographs on the following pages represent a small sample from my extensive portfolio. I own and operate a scenic photography gallery in Breckenridge, Colorado. I have hand-printed, matted, and framed all the images in this book many times over.

I hope you enjoy looking at these images as much as I did taking and printing them.

Collared Lizzard - Rabbit Ear Mesa near Fruita, Colorado

Late Afternoon - Maroon Bells framed by Aspen trees in Autumn color

Late Summer - wildflowers / Elk Range above Marble near McClure Pass

Horses - Aspen grove on Maroon Creek near Aspen

Wagon wheels, Aspen leaves above Buena Vista

Aspen - Bighorn Creek Trail above Vail

Trail above Maroon Lake - Autumn above Aspen

Fog - Lodgepole Pine forest / Genesee, near Denver

Aspen grove near Owl Creek Pass, Uncompahgre Range

Outlet - Upper Mohawk Lake above Breckenridge

Aspen, The Castles near Gunnison

Autumn on Molas Divide above Silverton

Bull Elk "bugling" to attract mate - Trail Ridge / Rocky Mountain National Park

Bright Red Indian Paintbrush above Vail Pass near Copper Mountain

Columbine - Yankee Boy Basin above Ouray

Continental Falls - Spruce Creek above Breckenridge

Wildflowers, North face of Quandary Peak near Breckenridge

2 Elk - early Summer snow, Rocky Mountain National Park

Fog, Spring snow - Aldifer Barn, Evergreen

Sunset - early Summer snow at Lake Dillon

Old barn, red Aspen above Last Dollar Road near Telluride

Columbine above Blue Lake near Breckenridge

Peak 8, Peak 7 - Breckenridge

Aspen in fog - Deluge Creek Trail above Vail

Aspen in snowstorm - Steamboat

Wildflowers below Blue Lakes Pass near Dallas Divide, San Juan Mountains

Aspen leaves - Ophir Pass above Silverton

Dusk, Mt. Baldy / Town of Breckenridge

Moonlight - Peak 8, Peak 7 / Breckenridge

Aspen - Mt. Gothic near Crested Butte

Storm aftermath - Monarch Ski Area

Early Summer - Crystal River Mill near Marble

Autumn - Crystal River Mill near Marble

Aspen leaves, Peak 1 near Frisco

Buffalo Peak from Sapphire Point, Lake Dillon

Hallett Peak, Rocky Mountain National Park

Maroon Bells from Aspen Highlands Ski Area

Indian Paintbrush - Fletcher Mountain near Breckenridge

Autumn - San Juan Mountains from Dallas Divide

Mt. Wilson - Aspen on Last Dollar Road near Telluride

Hoarfrost on Cottonwood near Ridgway

Mid-afternoon, Mt. Sneffels from Aspen Road above Ridgway

Late afternoon, Mt. Sneffels from Aspen Road above Ridgway

Aspen on Boreas Pass Road above Breckenridge

First snow on Ophir Pass above Silverton

Outlet - Lake Isabelle / Indian Peaks Wilderness near Nederland

Wildflowers - Yankee Boy Basin above Ouray

Cascades near Boothe Lake above Vail

Wildflowers near Capitol Peak above Snowmass

Pike's Peak from Garden of the Gods, Colorado Springs

Flatirons / Chatauqua Park, Boulder

Wildflowers on Shrine Ridge above Vail Pass

Wildflowers below Silver Creek Pass - Elk Range near Marble

Powder in the Aspens - Windows Run at Steamboat

Mount of the Holy Cross from the Back Bowls at Vail

Petroleum Lake above Lincoln Gulch near Aspen

Peak 10 from Peak 8 - Breckenridge

Columbine - Yankee Boy Basin above Ouray

Black Bear Pass above Silverton

Elk herd - Rocky Mountain National Park

Fog in the forest - Snowmass

Winter Panorama - Breckenridge

Keystone and Breckenridge from above Loveland Pass

Ancient Bristlecone Pines on Mt. Evans

Black Canyon of the Gunnison near Montrose

Narrow Gauge Georgetown Loop Railroad above Georgetown

Lupine near Crested Butte

Breckenridge from Keystone

Flocked Aspen, clearing storm - Breckenridge

Columbine, Indian Paintbrush - Imogene Pass above Ouray

Aspen grove - Snowmass

Columbine - American Basin near Lake City

Red Aspen - Molas Divide above Silverton

Wildflowers above Steamboat

Aspen - Long's Peak, Rocky Mountain National Park

Autumn - Pond above Maroon Lake - Maroon Bells near Aspen

Early Spring - outlet, Maroon Lake near Aspen

Golden Aspen on Boreas Pass Road above Breckenridge

North Peak at Keystone

Pacific Peak - Upper Mohawk Lake above Breckenridge

New York Range above Eagle

Aspen Road near Ridgway

San Juan Mountains from Dallas Divide above Ridgway

Aspen at Beaver Creek

Peak 8, Peak 7 - Breckenridge

Columbine and Indian Paintbrush - Black Bear Pass above Telluride

Ten Mile Range from Copper Mountain

Sunset - Continental Divide from Genesee

Sunset - Ten Mile Range, Lake Dillon

Storm - Ancient Bristlecone Pines on Windy Ridge above Alma

## PHOTOGRAPHER'S NOTES

**Cameras:**      MAMIYA RB-67 Pro-S ($2^1/_4$" x $2^3/_4$" negative size)

PENTAX 645 ($1^5/_8$" x $2^1/_4$")

FUJICA 645-S ($1^5/_8$" x $2^1/_4$")

HORSEMAN 612 with 6x7 back ($2^1/_4$" x $2^3/_4$")

BRONICA RF 645 ($1^5/_8$" x $2^1/_4$")


**Film:**      KODAK Kodacolor VR Gold ASA 100 / 120 Roll Size

FUJI Reala Superia ASA 100 / 120 Roll Size


**Paper:**      KODAK Supra III N-surface (for reproduction)


**Print Processor:**   KREONITE 26" Roller Transport


*If you wish to order original photographic prints of the images from this book*

*(in 5 different sizes, with matting and framing available), write us at:*

COLORADO SCENICS  124 S. Main Street  P. O. Box 5347  Breckenridge, CO 80424

or check our *WEBSITE:*  www.coloradoscenics.com

Sunset - Breckenridge

again. Bear in mind that heavy containers should be fitted with strong wheels like castors. However you intend to use container plants, a haphazard approach, dotting them randomly around the site, will not suit the image of the formal garden.

Certain container shapes have an affinity with particular plants, which might influence your choice, while there are more practical considerations to bear in mind when choosing containers for the modern formal garden. If planted earthenware is to be left out of doors, avoid narrow-necked shapes so that the 'frost heave' of the compost allows it to rise; be aware also that narrow necks make it impossible to remove large plants that have built up a huge rootball. For a large Ali Baba shape, the simple effect of a small trailing clematis, like *Clematis alpina* 'White Columbine', would be lovely in spring. Otherwise, vase shapes suit the fan effect of slim cordylines particularly well. Softer grassy forms, such as flowering pennisetums or hakonechloa foliage, combine well with glazed earthenware because of the textural contrast, while brown grasses like *Carex buchananii* are compatible with natural terracotta.

Geometric shapes with straight sides are particularly formal. They come in concrete, simulated stone, cast or imitation metals or timber. The vertical shapes of irises, tulips, lilies and *Nicotiana sylvestris* suit these, particularly if the pots are narrow and liable to be unbalanced by larger plants. Long, shallow troughs make good containers for the same type of plant, preferably planted as a linear mass without any extras to spoil the simplicity. Irises, sisyrinchiums and slim grasses like *Calamagrostis* x *acutiflora* 'Stricta' are all appropriate.

For practical reasons, statuesque plants need dignified containers, heavy enough to withstand wind. So square timber tubs, heavy stone containers or stainless steel cylinders will do a good job. Plants that emerge fully foliaged from ground level, like phormiums, suit a widening geometry but those that may be top-heavy, like standard clipped bays or marguerites, should be firmly based, relating them vertically to the ground.

Solo stars like dramatic fan palms, spiky yuccas, columnar conifers or small trees require sturdy and 'serious' containers. The shape should be simple to be effective, and should not compete with the plant. So if you are using timber, avoid the pastiche look of 'Versailles' ornamentation or anything with swags cast into the shape. Modern formal means clean-looking in every detail.

opposite below **On a sheltered balcony with redwood decking, permanent containers offer choice planting opportunities. Hardy fan palms fill four large white-painted wooden planters while the lower containers are used for summer annuals.**

below **Galvanized metal will not rust in water, making this trough ideal for aquatic marginal plants like Pontederia cordata. By late summer, blue flower spikes will adorn the arrow-shaped leaves.**

# index

Page numbers in *italic* refer to the illustrations

# acknowledgments

### Author's acknowledgments

I am full of admiration for the creativity of my garden design colleagues and enormously encouraged by the originality and sensitivity of the gardens shown in this book and photographed so perceptively.

I greatly appreciate the teamwork that is characteristic of Quadrille; this was led by Jane O'Shea with vision and constant encouragement throughout. I must particularly thank Carole McGlynn for her sustained clarity of thought and sensitivity when editing my text. The style of the book is due to Françoise Dietrich, who expresses its idiom so beautifully, and the artist Alison Barratt who eloquently interpreted my plans. Thanks are also due to Nadine Bazar for sourcing the superb photographs and to Jim Smith who tirelessly assembled the work with such good humour.

Finally I must thank my husband Bill for 'keeping the show on the road' at home, and my mother, Lilian Annis, for her understanding.

All illustrations by Alison Barratt

The publisher thanks the photographers and organizations for their kind permission to reproduce the following photographs in this book:

1 Andrew Wood; 2-3 Nicola Browne/design Steve Martino; 4 Karen Bussolini/design James David; 7 far left John Glover/design Alex Champion; 7 far right Nicola Browne/design Steve Martino; 7 left Marianne Majerus/design George Carter; 7 right Melanie Eclare/ design Tindale/Batstone Landscape Architects; 8-9 Deidi von Schaewen/ design Marc Brown; 10-11 Nicola Browne/ design Faith Okuma; 12-13 Nicola Browne/design Steve Martino; 14-15 Nicola Browne/design Steve Martino; 16 left Marianne Majerus/design Marc Schoellen; 16 right Photo Clarisse/design Philippe Niez; 17 Woods Bagot/design Nik Karalis; 18 above David Buurma; 18 below Jill Billington/design Christina Dalnoky; 19 Michael Moran/design Billie Tsien Associates; 20 Deidi von Schaewen; 21 left Clive Nichols/design David Stevens; 21 right David Buurma; 23 left Jill Billington; 23 right Nicola Browne/design Andrew Cao; 24 left Nicola Browne/design Bonita Bulaitis; 24 right John Glover/design Anglo Aquarium; 25 Lanny Provo; 26 Jill Billington/design Fogg, Bulaitis & Santer; 27 left Andrew Wood/Chaumont Festival; 27 right Jerry Harpur/design Juan Grimm; 28 Jill Billington/design Charles Jencks; 29 Andrew Lawson/design Kathy Swift; 30 left Marianne Majerus/design Vivien Fowler & Tom Jestico; 30 right Andrew Wood/design Stephen Woodhams; 31 The Interior Archive/Henry Wilson/design Ian Chee; 33 left The Interior Archive/Herbert Ypma/design Yturba; 33 right Mark Bolton; 34 Dan Kiley; 35 centre Nicola Browne/design Jinny Blom; 35 left Photo Clarisse/Chaumont Festival; 35 right Andrew Wood/Chaumont Festival; 36 Jerry Harpur/design Topher Delaney San Francisco; 37 above Marianne Majerus/design Julia Brett; 37 below Colin Philp/design Jill Billington; 38-39 Melanie Eclare/design Niall Manning & Alastair Morton; 40 Geoff Lung/design Richard Unsworth; 41 Andrew Wood; 42 left Marianne Majerus/design Stephen Woodhams; 42 centre & right Andrew Wood; 43 Melanie Eclare/design Tindale/Batstone Landscape Architects; 45 left Photo Clarisse/design Sylvie Devinat; 45 right Jerry Harpur/design Isabelle Greene; 46 Reiner Blunck/design Gabriele Poole; 47 left Katherine Spitz; 47 right Jerry Harpur/design Juan Grimm; 48 Vladimir Sitta/Terragram Pty Ltd; 49 left Andrew Wood; 49 right Jerry Harpur/design Topher Delaney San Francisco; 50 left Andrew Wood/Chaumont Festival; 50 right Andrew Wood/design Stephen Woodhams; 51 Jerry Harpur/design Dyruff; 52 Lanny Provo; 53 above The Interior Archive/Herbert Ypma; 53 below Garden Picture Library/Mayer/Le Scanff; 54 Clive Nichols/design Paul Thompson & Trevyn McDowell; 55 left Robert O'Dea; 55 right Jerry Harpur/design Topher Delaney San Francisco; 56 centre The Interior Archive/Helen Fickling; 56 left Melanie Eclare/design Niall Manning & Alastair Morton; 56 right Jerry Harpur/design Topher Delaney San Francisco; 57 Marianne Majerus/design Jill Billington; 58 Andrea Jones; 59 Nicola Browne/design Martha Schwartz; 60 left Clive Nichols/design Hiroshi Namamori; 60 right Jerry Harpur/design Robert Liang; 61 Nicola Browne/design Martha Schwartz; 62-63 Karen Bussolini/design James David; 64 above Deidi von Schaewen; 64 below Andrew Lawson/design David Hicks; 65 Photo Clarisse/design Yves Gosse de Gorre; 66 left Clive Nichols/design Christopher Bradley-Hole; 66 right Marianne Majerus/design Tessa Hobbs/obelisk design George Carter; 67 Christine Ternynck/design Piet Blanckaert; 68 above Mark Bolton; 68 below Jerry Harpur/design Luciano Giubbilei; 69 Marianne Majerus/design George Carter; 71 above Jill Billington; 71 below Stephen Jerrom/design Andrew Cao; 72 Jerry Harpur/design Isabelle Greene; 73 left Andrew Wood/design Stephen Woodhams; 73 right Mick Hales/Greenworld Pictures; 74 above S & O Mathews; 74 below Clive Nichols/Huntingtron Botanic Gardens; 75 Photo Clarisse/Chaumont Festival; 76 above Karen Bussolini/design Richard Bergmann; 76 below Jerry Harpur/design Isabelle Greene; 77 Jerry Harpur/ design Isabelle Greene; 78 above Marianne Majerus/design Michelle Osbourne; 78 below Andrew Wood/design Stephen Woodhams; 79 Clive Nichols/design David Hicks; 80 Photo Clarisse; 81 View/Dennis Gilbert/design Munkenbeck & Marshall; 82 left Stephen Jerrom/design Andrew Cao; 82 right Jerry Harpur/design Edwina von Gal; 83 Marianne Majerus/design Arabella Lennox-Boyd; 84 Mick Hales/Greenworld Pictures/design Beebe Yodell; 85 John Glover/design Christopher Bradley-Hole; 86 left Nicola Browne/Arends Nursery; 86 right Arcaid/Richard Bryant; 87 John Glover; 88-89 Marianne Majerus/ design Jacques Wirtz; 90 Mark Schwartz/design Ron Herman; 92 Andrew Lawson/design Anthea Gibson; 93 Karen Bussolini/design Richard Bergmann; 94 above Christine Ternynck; 94 below Jill Billington/design Charles Jencks; 96 Karen Bussolini/design Richard Bergmann; 97 above Tim Harvey/design Martha Schwartz; 97 below Deidi von Schaewen/design Marc Brown; 98 Melanie Eclare/design Niall Manning & Alastair Morton; 99 above Ian Pleeth/design Jill Billingon; 99 below Deidi von Schaewen; 100 far left, above & below Andrew Wood; 100 centre Photo Clarisse; 102 Jean-Pierre Gabriel/design Daniël Ost; 103 above Jerry Harpur/design Terry Welch; 103 below Jill Billington/design Cleve West; 104 Marianne Majerus/design George Carter; 106 Andrew Lawson/design James Aldridge; 107 Jill Billington/design Dan Pearson; 108 Marijke Heuff; 109 Jerry Harpur/design Daniel Gaboulaud; 110 Melanie Eclare/design Niall Manning & Alastair Morton; 111 Clive Nichols/design George Carter; 112 above Jean-Pierre Gabriel/design Erik Dhont; 112 below John Glover/design Alex Champion; 114 Jill Billington/design Bonita Bulaitis; 115 Marijke Heuff; 116 above Marianne Majerus/design Julia Brett; 116 below David Buurma; 117 Deidi von Schaewen/ design Jack Lenor Larson; 118 Photo Clarisse/Chaumont Festival; 119 Andrew Lawson/design Tom Sitta; 120 Marianne Majerus; 121 Jean-Pierre Gabriel/design Daniël Ost; 122 Marianne Majerus; 123 Marianne Majerus/design Marc Schoellen; 125 above John Glover/design Jill Billington & Barbara Hunt; 125 below Marianne Majerus/ design Jill Billington & Barbara Hunt; 126 Marianne Majerus/design Jill Billington & Barbara Hunt; 127 above Andrew Wood/design Stephen Woodhams; 127 below Jerry Harpur/design Isabelle Greene; 128 Photo Clarisse; 130 above Christian Sarramon; 130 below Santi Caleca; 131 Mark Schwartz/ design Ron Herman; 132 left Belle/Trevor Mein; 132 right Andrew Wood; 133 Jerry Harpur/design Topher Delaney San Francisco; 134 Nicola Browne/design Steve Martino; 135 Jerry Harpur/design Topher Delaney; 136 Garden Picture Library/Steve Wooster/design Michelle Osbourne; 137 above Arcaid/Richard Bryant/design Seth Stein; 137 below Tim Harvey/design Martha Schwartz; 139 above Andrew Wood/Chaumont Festival; 139 below Marianne Majerus/ design George Carter; 140 Jean-Pierre Gabriel/design Erik Dhont; 141 Andrea Jones/design Paul Thompson & Trevyn McDowell; 142 John Glover /design Tim Brown; 143 Arcaid/Richard Bryant/design Seth Stein; 145 left Mark Schwartz/ design Ron Herman; 145 right Jerry Harpur/design Luciano Giubbilei; 146 Jerry Harpur/design Isabelle Greene; 147 above Clive Nichols/design Paul Thompson & Trevyn McDowell; 147 below Andrew Wood/Chaumont Festival; 148 Andrew Wood/Chaumont Festival; 150 Clive Nichols/design Victor Shanley; 151 Marijke Heuff; 152 Derek St Romaine/design Wynniatt-Husey Clarke; 153 Andrew Wood/design Stephen Woodhams; 154 left Photo Clarisse; 154 right Marianne Majerus/design Diana Yakeley; 155 Andrew Wood/Chaumont Festival; 156 above Mark Bolton/Chaumont Festival; 156 below Andrew Lawson/design Anthony Noel; 157 Andrew Wood/Chaumont Festival.